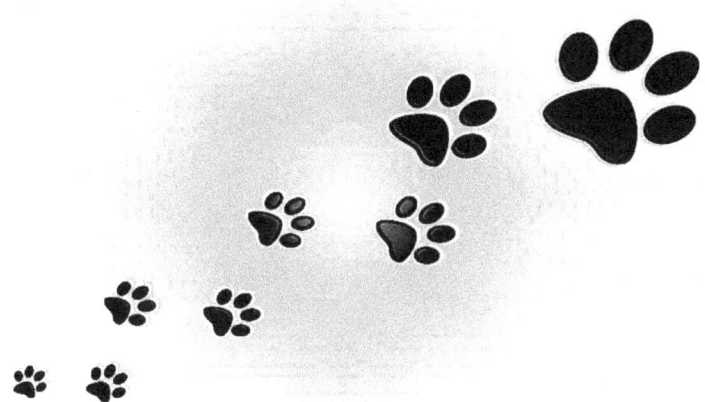

The Puddin' Diaries

An entirely true and unexpected journey through puppyhood and healing.

Kimberly J. Johnston

*This book is dedicated to Alena and Brady.
Never stop chasing your dreams!
Nothing is impossible!
LYTTMAB
~Mom~*

~Chapter One~

My name is Kim. I am a divorced mother of two outrageously funny two-legged children, Alena (12 years old) and Brady (4 years old); and now one very precocious four-legged child named Puddin'. We live in a small house, in a small town in the great state of Texas. The name Puddin' is pronounced similar to pudding, but throw on a bit of Texas twang on the end...hence, the missing 'g'.

Well, here's how the story goes. My daughter is quite the animal lover and has been begging me to get a dog for months. Our last pet, Snuggles, passed away three years ago and Alena has been completely lost without a four-legged companion ever since.

Just recently being divorced, I'm still adjusting to the life of a single working mom on a fixed income with very limited "free" time. Quite frankly, the idea of a dog could make me feel the need to pour myself a tall, stiff, adult beverage; and I don't even drink!

So one day, September 30th, to be exact, our lives took an unexpected turn. Whether it was for the worse or the better is yet to be determined. My ex-husband has a lovely new girlfriend. And I mean lovely with all sincerity. She is a lovely woman and I'm just tickled that he has found someone so wonderful. But this story isn't about that. It's about a dog.

The girlfriend went out to her truck on this morning and found a sweet puppy, with no collar or tags cowering under the vehicle. Later that afternoon, the ex-husband sent a picture text of the puppy to Alena saying, "Look what we found". Well, needless to say Alena was very concerned about where the dog came from, what they were going to do with the dog, and then...I knew it was coming...I braced myself. "Momma can we keep her?" The voice inside my head screamed- not only no, but heck no! But who can resist a brown-eyed girl and a puppy?

The long and short of it is that the girlfriend is not able to have pets at her rental property so the dog would _have_ to go to a shelter if we didn't take her. For Alena, that was unacceptable. So, off we went to meet the dog. She didn't have a name yet so she was just "the dog". The agreement was she could stay one night until we figured out what to do or until someone claimed her.

It was love at first sight for the kids, including Brady who is not an animal lover. For me, it was panic and a little bit of contempt for the ex and the girlfriend. I'd been set up...totally!

I had never seen a green-eyed dog before. The big floppy ears did kind of melt my heart just a bit until I saw her feet. Oh my word! Look at those paws! This dog is going to be **HUGE**! Big dog means big messes and who's going to clean all of that up? Nope this is NOT happening to me.

We loaded the dog in the car and off we went to track down some puppy food for our one-night arrangement. Within five minutes of our car ride, this is what I hear from my non-animal lover, Brady- my only ally and my last hope of not keeping the dog; "I think we call her

Puddin' 'cause she reminds me of chocolate and banilla pudding". I was sunk. All hope was lost. The kids had named her. There was no turning back now. If no one claimed her we would have a dog.

And, so began the comedy of errors that my life is now characterized by. But also began a journey of healing and growth that I was quite unprepared for.

~Chapter Two~

Being completely unprepared for a puppy, we made do with what we had the first night at home. Chew toys were made out of socks with knots tied in them. The water and food bowls were previously used as cereal bowls. Snuggles' old blankets were pulled out of the hope chest for the new addition to our family.

The kids sat in the living room with Puddin' and played with her while I sank into my chair with a million questions and no answers. *How in the heck did this happen? I mean, after all I have white carpet and she's a puppy. I have a job thirty-six miles away. I have joint custody of my two-legged children, who is going to take care of this dog when they aren't home? How am I going to afford this? God, what message are you trying to deliver to me; how is this ever going to work?*

Puddin' and Alena were best friends from the word, 'go'. She followed Alena everywhere she went. When Alena went into her room to go to bed, Puddin' jumped onto the bed and laid down right beside her and fell asleep within minutes. After all, I suppose getting lost and then found is pretty stressful when you're a puppy.

Night One- Puddin' slept in Alena's bed until about 3:00 a.m. We had a few potty accidents in the house, but that's part of puppies I suppose. She didn't bark, wander or cause any trouble, until the morning.

Did I mention that Puddin' is extremely skittish? She does not like going outside- hence the potty accidents in the house. If she hears any kind of noise, she tucks her tail and bolts under the bed; between someone's legs; under the pillows on the bed- anywhere she can hide. She's scared of everything! So when I started to blow dry my hair that morning, she barked and growled at me from the doorway of the bathroom.

While I'm drying my hair I'm trying to decide what I'm going to do with Puddin' during the day while I'm at work and the kids are at school. I decide at least for day one she could stay in the bathroom until lunchtime when the ex agreed to check on her for me. I figured I could go buy a crate; puppy food; a collar; a leash; treats; and dog shampoo on my lunch break. Yep, that was the plan.

Brady woke up at 5:00 a.m. to play with Puddin'. He did not want to go to school and explained, "She'll be sad without me mommy." I laughed that he was already so concerned for the dog. Especially after last night when she tried to crawl into bed with him and he yelled: "Puddin' this is my bed- go to Alena's room!"

I prepare the bathroom. I take the toilet paper off the roller so we can't play the puppy toilet paper game. If you've ever had puppies, you know what I'm talking about. If you haven't, let me explain. The puppy grabs the end of the toilet paper roll and proceeds to run with it, pulling all of the toilet paper off the roll and all over your floor. It's quite a mess. The only upside to the game is _if_ they have a potty accident, it's usually on top of the unrolled toilet paper so it's easy to clean up. From what I hear, very few puppies make it into adult dog-hood without playing this game at least once.

Toilet paper off the roll and onto the counter- check; cereal bowl with some water in it- check; sock with knot tied in it- check; blanket on the floor for her to lay on- check; small desk fan plugged in and on the counter for air circulation- check; toilet lid down so she can't drown- check; lights on so she doesn't get scared- check; shower curtain pinned up where she can't get to it- check; soaps and shampoos up out of puppy's reach- check. Ok, I think I've covered everything.

Well as my momma would say, "if it can go wrong, it will!" It appears, lil' miss Puddin' has some separation anxiety. When the ex-husband got there to check on her around lunchtime Puddin' had gotten up onto the bathroom counter; turned off the light and turned on the hot water in the sink. In addition, she pooped on the counter <u>and</u> on the kid's toothbrushes; knocked over a vase with flowers in it; knocked the fan onto the floor and knocked her water bowl over. Thankfully, the fan came unplugged when she knocked it down otherwise the dog would've fried with all the water.

The ex calls me saying the dog and the bathroom are completely covered in poop and that it smelled terrible because the bathroom had steamed up from all the hot water running with the door closed. He spent his lunch break cleaning her up. He petted her for a little while and then improvised on re-pinning her for the afternoon. As I'm hearing him describe the scene he walked into, I can't help but grin from ear-to-ear. The upside to a destroyed bathroom- my ex had to clean poop off a dog. Yes, vengeance is sweet indeed.

My lunch break comes and it's off to the pet store for supplies. Note to self: kids need new toothbrushes. I walked into the local pet store and apparently I must have had a very lost look on my face. A nice young man came up and asked what I was looking for. So I explained how Puddin' had joined our family *temporarily* and that I was completely unprepared for a puppy but that I was also a single mom on a very fixed income.

God works in some not so mysterious ways sometimes. This nice young man found a crate; dog bowls; collar; leash and dog shampoo all on his clearance rack. He also threw in some puppy treats and a ball for free. Feeling incredibly grateful we get to the cash register and I'm praying that I haven't just broken the bank. He rings everything up and my heart sinks when I see the total. But then he pulls out a coupon book and starts scanning. I watch the total drop a bit, but it's still over my budget. He looks at me and says, "Lady here- we're going to use my discount on all this stuff. After all, you did rescue the pooch." And in a rapid succession of keystrokes, my total was now under $90 and I could live with that.

I make one more stop for toothbrushes, room spray and candles, as I'm sure I'll need them. The ex may have cleaned up the dog but not the bathroom. Back to work I go with a trunk full of necessities for night number two. Hey wait a minute! Wasn't this a one-night arrangement?

Night two I bring home all of the goodies for Puddin'. Brady decides to help me put the crate together. The man at the pet store assured me it would be easy; "it just pops right up", he said. Well, I'm here to tell ya'- it didn't!

There was a broken fingernail involved and some collateral cussing and crying on account of the broken fingernail; which resulted in eruptions of laughter from my peanut gallery. As soon as the crate was together- Puddin' gathered all of her toys, including the knot tied socks scattered throughout the house and took them all into the crate and laid down.

Day two was relatively uneventful when compared to day one. Your typical puppy drama- they eat, sleep, chew and potty. The ex informed me she seemed really happy in her crate and that she had no accidents in it and climbed right back in after their mid-day romp and potty break.

Day two rolls to an end and I decide I better call a veterinarian and see if by miracle of chances, she has a microchip. If not and if she's going to stay with us, I guess I better get her checked out. I find a veterinarian in town that offered a FREE, (my favorite word by far in this experience), exam. Besides, we have to figure out what kind of dog she is so we know what to expect right? The kids are great at loving on her and playing with her. However, cleaning up after her is mom's job…sadly for me.

Day three and Puddin' weeds out a man I had been spending my free time with. He apparently was not fond of dogs and absolutely did not believe that dogs belonged in the house, much less in a human's bed. I politely asked him if he was giving me an ultimatum of choosing between him and the dog. Well, Puddin' won and the "boy" is no longer in the picture. I decided if he was jealous of a dog I could only imagine if he ever got to meet my children! No thank you- next!

The following days mirrored that of bringing home a newborn baby. My life now revolved around when Puddin' needed to eat, sleep and potty. I'm exhausted from waking up in the middle of the night to take her out and a part of me is begging for her owners to come and claim her.

The morning of Puddin's appointment with the veterinarian we attempt to put her on a leash to take her in the car. It reminded me of a hog being tied. She did not like the leash and we ended up carrying her.

There was no microchip discovered, which resulted in Alena sobbing. I asked her what was wrong and she said, "mom, that means she's really ours now". As if that statement alone didn't solidify Puddin's place in our home, the bill at the end of the visit was the nail in the coffin. The exam was in fact free, but the vaccinations were not.

We learned that Puddin' is approximately a 4-month old Pit Bull mix that by all signs is perfectly healthy. No ticks; fleas; ear mites; worms or the like. She weighed in right around 20 pounds and we can expect her to grow to between 70 and 80 pounds.

She has some abandonment issues; social anxiety and we need to work with her. Oh great! Not only do I now have a dog I wasn't planning on, I have a dog with 'issues'! Are you kidding me God? I have enough 'issues' of my own now I have to deal with the dog's? Between the two of us we now have enough 'issues' for an entire lifetime subscription. How did this happen to me? God and I have had many conversations since Puddin' joined our family. Most of the time, it's me praying for patience and strength.

~Chapter Three~

The days after the veterinarian appointment were comprised of me accepting Puddin's presence in our lives. She is easy to love and really is a great companion to me when the kids aren't home. She occupies my time and keeps me laughing.

Acceptance doesn't happen overnight however. It's a process. We get frustrated with each other. I can show my frustration by raising my voice just ever so slightly and she tucks her tail and runs. She can show her frustration with me by eating my shoes. We need to work on our communication if this relationship is ever going to work.

In addition to accepting that we now have a puppy, we have had to learn to accept the negative comments people have when they find out she's a Pit Bull mix. Unfortunately, the breed has a terrible reputation for being aggressive. Well, if you've met Puddin' you know that's absolutely NOT the case with her.

Dog parks; apartment complexes; hotels; pet boarding facilities and even insurance companies have restrictions and rules about Pit Bulls. Alena has done quite a bit of research and the more we learn, the more we realize that aggression, although somewhat a personality or breed specific trait, is more often times a learned behavior. Playtime, cuddling, love and affection are all ways to help deter that.

We don't use corporal punishment with Puddin'. Aggression begets aggression. We use rewards for good behavior and discourage bad behavior by changing the pitch and tone of our voices. She's smart as a whip and has learned to sit on command; responds to the word, 'no'; and is slowly figuring out that her potty business belongs outside.

Puddin' is quite protective of the kids. She rarely barks unless its play time. But in the middle of the night if she hears something- she takes position in the hallway between the kid's rooms and barks ferociously to make her presence known. Of course this barking in the middle of the night results in a chorus of, "Puddin' be quiet!" from all of us as we roll over agitated to try and go back to sleep. Meanwhile, it's up to mom to get up and see what the commotion is and calm the dog back down. It's usually a car driving by outside or the wind blowing through the trees. Any kind of noise in the night warrants the sounding of the "Puddin' siren".

I laugh realizing that this big ole' bad Pit Bull sounds incredibly ferocious and vicious and would make someone think twice about coming into my house uninvited, but if they only knew she was scared of everything! Not to mention, her name is Puddin'!

When people ask us what kind of dog she is, we usually just respond with, "she's a mutt". It avoids the looks wherein people question my parenting by having such "an aggressive breed" in the house with my children. Most people that say bad things about the breed are uneducated or misinformed and are speaking strictly based on news stories they've heard or read- not on actual firsthand experience. If you've met our dog, then you would know, she's as loveable as they come and is more interested in licking you to death than attacking you.

The process of acceptance and adjusting our life for Puddin' is ever constant. We learn from experiences of what we can and cannot do with puppy in the house. We've learned that shoes cannot be in sight or in reach or they are subject to being annihilated. We've learned that you can however leave a plate of people food on the table and she will not even attempt to steal a bite. Sticks are meant to be eaten, as is anything else made of wood.

~Chapter Four~

Revenge is sweet, so they say. I'd like to know who "they" are and what makes them so dang smart. We need to rewind a few years for you to get the full picture of the rest of our story.

We have a family friend named Pat. Pat is an animal lover, just like Alena. Many years ago another friend of mine found a puppy on the side of a highway. For whatever reason, and I cannot for the life of me remember what the reason was, we weren't able to keep this puppy. So I went to her house with this little puppy in my arms hoping she'd take him in.

Well, that was more than six years ago and Bear is still a member of Pat's family. Although, Pat wasn't as lucky as we were with Puddin. Bear had fleas, ear mites and worms. Getting him healthy cost Pat a small fortune.

When Puddin' joined our lives, I started emailing Pat and my mom all about our experiences with a puppy in the house and those emails were titled, "The Puddin' Diaries", hence the name of this book. After about a month of emails being passed around, friends and family came to me and said, "Kim, these are too good- you need to write a book." So, here we are.

The rest of these chapters are a compilation of those original emails.

~Chapter Five~

Brady has decided that he wants Puddin' to be a boy instead of a girl. I explained that God made Puddin' a girl and that we couldn't change how God made her. He insists she needs to be a boy! And then, last night he asked if God could please make Puddin' stop eating his Transformers, especially since God didn't make her a boy! Ahh, the innocence of youth.

The great part of having Puddin' in the house is that she has made my kids pick up after themselves. They've lost a few valuable treasures in the past week from leaving them out where she can get them. A lesson I've tried to teach them for years and in one week, the dog nails it! Yes, I'm a bit resentful about this.

Last night Alena and I took Puddin' out for her last potty break of the evening. While we were out, Brady decided it made really good sense to shut and lock the back door, and in doing so, locked all the "girls" out of the house. Alena and I started banging on the door trying to get him to come unlock it. Finally, after about 3 minutes of yelling and banging, he came within view with his arms crossed across his chest, just grinning from ear-to-ear. I tried the usual, "Seth Braden if you don't open this door right now..." He turned and walked away! Can you believe that? He came back and Alena promised him ice cream if he would unlock the door. So Alena saves the day- woo hoo! He unlocked the door and RAN to hide. Puddin' found him first and started licking him from head to toe, which he did not like at all so I figure that was punishment enough.

Puddin' is putting some weight on- the little piglet. She is finally no longer afraid of the crickets and has even tried to eat one or two. The frogs from the creek bed still make her whine, tuck her tail and run however. Progress! At least we have conquered the crickets.

Alena got her to walk to the end of the front yard on her leash this weekend, which is an improvement from the driveway last week. She still tucks and runs if a car drives by and whimpers loudly if she sees someone she doesn't know. She has an aversion to blondes and barks fiercely at them…not sure what that's about. Although, she did let sweet Mrs. Stewart walk all the way up to her the other day and pet her without jumping, barking or whining. She just sat and waited, wagging her tail. They say dogs are good judges of character. Well, Mrs. Stewart is about the sweetest person I know, so I believe it!

She loves her crate and it has become her little sanctuary. When she's had enough of the kids, she retreats to her crate. The kids know to leave her alone if she's in her crate. I've explained to them that's her way of saying, "I'm done for now".

We're still having accidents in the house. But, Rome wasn't built in a day, or so the saying goes. So we just keep cleaning up, lighting candles and keep the carpet shampoo on the ready.

~Chapter Six~

Puddin' and I reluctantly resort to sleeping together in my room instead of Alena's when she's not home. I say reluctantly because I am always reluctant to share my bed with the farting, snoring, legs twitching in her sleep, dog. It reminds me of why I got divorced...just kidding...ok not really....maybe...

Bedtime. There's about 4 minutes of bouncing around on the bed, some playful barking, pulling at the blankets, moving the pillows to where she wants them, circle-circle-circle, give mom unwanted kisses on the face. HEY! WOW! WAIT A MINUTE! Who's that dog in the mirror? Bark-bark-bark; growl; tilt head from side-to-side; bark-bark-bark; back up on top of mom and drop head into the "attack" position. Me: "Stupid dog, that's your own reflection- stop barking at yourself!" Puddin: "Ruff!" So the mystery of the dog in the mirror is over and we can finally go to bed. Oh wait! She realizes she doesn't have her 'sock' so off she goes to retrieve it. The 'sock' is one with a knot tied in it that we made for her to play with her first night with us. Since then, it goes everywhere with her and we've actually made about 5 of them and they are hidden all over the house.

Off she goes to retrieve it. She brings it back, running and sliding down the hallway. She has not figured out that you can't stop when you are running full speed on wood floor. I hear the slide as I yell, "slow down!!!" And as she tries to stop to turn the corner into my room- WABAM! Right into the wall.

Me: "Puddin' I told you to slow down!" She stands up-shakes it off and starts running again. Only she can't exactly get traction on the wood so it's kind of like running in place. But then, she gets her footing and lunges onto the bed, using my stomach as a landing pad, back to her spot.

She stays in her spot next to me for about 2 minutes while I rub her belly. Then I roll over to go to sleep. This is when the fun begins. She sneaks to the top of the bed where my head is and wiggles her way underneath my pillow. Yes, the one my head is laying on. So now, I'm laying on a dog, under a pillow, under my head. This is not comfortable. I move-she moves and we do this dance for about another 3 minutes until one of us finally gives up...usually me.

Remember I said she farts? Well, with her body now underneath my head I am awakened thinking something has died in my bedroom! Only to be disgusted by the fact that she farted on my pillow! So I grab another pillow, bury my face in it and try to go back to sleep.

12:30a.m.: I get awakened by a tongue across the face; paws on my chest and a wiggling tail that is shaking the entire bed. This is her way of telling me I have less than 1 minute to get her outside before she pees! So out we go. We have to scope the patio for frogs or anything else potentially hazardous...then there's a big stretch...all the while I'm standing in the grass freezing waiting for this lovely creature God has made and blessed me with to do her business!

Finally, success! Hallelujah I can go back to sleep. We go back into the house and it's a race back to my bed to claim the warm spot. Since she has four legs and I only have two, she usually wins and lays right in my spot. So now, it's a fight for who's laying where.

5:00a.m.: the alarm goes off and Puddin' howls and jumps around on the bed. This is about the time I realize she's had an accident in the house- even AFTER the middle of the night trip outside. I could handle the accidents if I wasn't getting up in the middle of the night to take her out. But why oh why can't she wake me up the next time she needs to go? She woke me up the first time! Ugh!

She has breakfast while I get in the shower. She comes to visit and likes to pull the shower curtain back so she can see me. It's not a pretty sight I'm sure. Maybe that's why she's traumatized- she's seen me naked one too many times. Hmmm, do they have therapy for dogs?

We hustle to get ready and it's time for me to put on my shoes. I sit down on the side of the bed to put my shoes on. While I'm putting one on- she grabs the other and runs down the hall. So now, I'm yelling, chasing the dog with one shoe on my foot and the other one on the lamb. And I wonder why I'm so tired al the time!

Pat, all I can say is that I'm so very sorry for dropping Bear off on your door all those years ago. Are we even yet? Please...

~Chapter Seven~

Someone asked me recently how long we have had Puddin'. And all I could say, while trying to smile, was that it felt like she had been a part of the family forever. Last night we confronted a frog in the grass, quite by accident.

We were going out to do our business. She will not step off the patio unless you walk into the grass with her. She's a bit of a pansy. So there we were- walking in the grass and she was sniffing things out when a frog leapt towards her...

BATTLE STATIONS! WOOP! WOOP! WOOP! ALARM! WARNING!

She jumped backwards, laid her ears completely back and then jumped into my arms. Now, when I say jumped - I mean it quite literally. She jumped so high that all I had to do was put my arms out to catch her. So there I am, holding this big ole' bad 25+ pound pit bull in my arms. Aggressive breed my butt!

I am laughing and wishing I had a camera. She lays her head on my shoulder with her nose tucked up under my hair. Me: "Puddin' it's just a frog it won't hurt you- come one let's go see it". I bend down, still holding the mutt in my arms so that she can make nice with Mr. Frog, from the creek, in the yard.

Well, at least that was my plan. As I bend down, she claws her way up my chest-over my shoulder and uses my back as a launch pad and jumps towards the patio. She runs up the steps and sits down in front of the door, looking back at me. So much for going potty- thanks Mr. Frog- you've just guaranteed I'll be cleaning up yet another mess in the house tonight. I hate frogs.

Bedtime was the normal routine. Although I mistakenly left my flip-flops on the floor by the back door and they are now another casualty in the Puddin' Puppy War. I guess I should practice what I keep preaching to the kids.

I did discover this morning that if I sing loudly in the shower she will do one of two things: she'll either howl along with me or she runs and hides under my bed with only a wagging tail sticking out.

I love this dog!

~Chapter Eight~

Maybe I should write a book. After all, you can't make this kind of stuff up! After almost a month of having Puddin' in our lives- I can't even look at a package of pudding at the grocery store without laughing.

Brady loves Puddin' but has very strict rules and boundaries with her. In other words, she is NOT allowed in his room under any circumstances...EVER. In fact, there is a sign on Brady's door, although invisible to the world- he expects it to be visible to the dog, as he informed her yesterday morning, and I quote: "Puddin' you see this- it says NO DOGS ALLOWED!" And then he proceeded to walk away, leaving the door open.

Now Puddin' is a bit rebellious and I guess she decided she would test that sign. So into Brady's room she sneaks to grab a toy to prove she's been in there and then she RRRRRRRUUUUUUUUUNNNNNNNNSSSS with it in her mouth; making a pass by Brady on the couch so he can see her treasure; into the kitchen and out the back door!

This results in some screaming of the dog's name and begging mommy to please save the toy. So off I go chasing Puddin' in the back yard in hair rollers and my robe with Brady and Alena in close pursuit behind me. After all, they don't want to miss anything. Have you ever tried to catch a dog? Again, she has four legs, I only have two. It is inevitable that I am NEVER going to win and yet because my sweet baby boy is having a fit, I have to try and do the impossible.

All the while, I'm mumbling and cussing under my breath wondering how I ever ended up with a dog in the first place!

Finally she pauses long enough for me to bend over to retrieve the toy and off like a rocket she goes again. This makes my pre-teen laugh loudly at her mother who is now furiously yelling, "Puddin'" at the top of her lungs with her robe now flapping in the wind exposing all of her goodies for anyone and everyone to see. Thank you Jesus the neighbors aren't out!

It is at this moment as I re-tie up my robe, listening to my daughter's cackling- I am reminded of exactly how this dog came into our lives- Alena! So guess what? Mom's fed up and Alena wanted the dog- so guess who gets to chase the dog to retrieve Brady's most prized possession? FYI- whatever toy Puddin' has stolen becomes his most prized possession. That will show her not to laugh at her half-naked mother chasing the dog.

This, "I've had it-it's your dog- it's your problem" moment usually results in some eye rolling and a, "What did I do" attitude from my sweet oldest child. Which causes some "Don't you dare take that tone with me young lady...blah, blah, blah". All the while baby brother has apparently lost interest in his most favorite toy and is back inside on the couch with his chocolate milk watching cartoons. Alena and I exchange glances and wonder, why in the heck are we chasing this dog?

After all, it is Brady's fault for leaving the door open in the first place and it is HIS toy we're trying to save. Puddin'- 1; Humans-0.

Why we can't get out the door on time in the mornings? Why I'm absolutely exhausted by the time I start my car to leave for work.

~Chapter Nine~

I surveyed the damage of the Puddin' Puppy War, the 'PPW' as we now call it, this morning. I stood there with coffee cup in hand amidst the dew covered grass- which by the way also frightens the dog...she's not sure what to think of it.

My backyard looks like a mass casualty incident of little green army men; a few chewed-up Legos here and there; a now unidentifiable object that I'm sure at one point was something of great importance; a pair of socks (not matching by the way); and one...one lonely pale green house slipper. They were once my favorite and now, it's missing sole; busted strap and mud covered body are just too tragic to look at, it's MIA or perhaps, we must assume it was killed in the line of duty...tragedy and despair.

Everywhere I look I see destruction and devastation. How did this happen? How did it ever come to this? And then I see the green-eyed monster responsible for it all- Puddin'.

I shake my head and we begin yet another day.

~Chapter Ten~

I love this dog! I've decided God brought her into my life to keep me laughing and to teach me lessons in patience and tolerance because apparently even thought I am raising kids, I am not learning those lessons fast enough.

So you haven't seen my kitchen drain situation so I'll try to describe it as best I can. The kitchen sink and dishwasher drain through an open hole in the side of the concrete, on the side of the house, onto the back patio and runs off into the grass. It's an old house. This hole is about 2 inches across- just big enough for one Puddin' nose.

Last night I was on the back patio with the dog for her to go potty. If I'll sit out there she'll venture into the grass by herself now. We are making progress, be it ever so slowly.

I'm sitting enjoying the peaceful night air waiting for the dog to do her business when my peacefulness is interrupted by some muffled growling and claws scraping on the concrete. I look around to find Puddin' with her nose halfway lodged in the drain. I panic a bit because I'm not sure how stuck she is and in my mind I'm picturing the bill from the Fire Department to come dislodge my dog! You know me- worst case scenario. That and jumping to conclusions are after all the only exercise I get, other than chasing Puddin'.

I digress. I jump up and start talking to her so she knows its me walking up behind her. I put my hands around her mid-section and try to pull her back gently- not wanting to hurt her. No luck! She's wiggling too much. If she'd keep her head still, I'm quite certain she could've figured her way out. But alas, she was panicked and kept moving her head from side to side. I had to be a bit more forceful with her and grab her around the neck with one hand to hold her head still while trying to pull her free. I pull a little harder and out she popped and back on my butt I fell. No blood, no scratches, not a mark on her. My butt however, was aching from landing on the concrete.

She shook her head from side to side and sat down staring at the drain. I cleaned off her snout and loved on her for a minute. When I got up to resume my seat on the patio (because we still hadn't gone potty), she walked away turned her head toward the drain and gave it a "ruff" before running off to play.

~Chapter Eleven~

Potty training a puppy should be compared to beating your head against a wall. Although you nail down a routine and you schedule your entire life around when the dang dog needs to potty, accidents are bound to happen. After all, they are puppies and are still learning right? Well try explaining this to a four-year-old.

I mentioned that Puddin' is not allowed in Brady's room- EVER. Well, Brady has a bad habit of leaving his bedroom door open. Puddin', being the defiant little creature that she is, likes to sneak in there from time to time and do her business. This morning, an exasperated Brady had a heart to heart with a very naughty Puddin'. As I was coming out of my bedroom, this is what I heard: Brady: "Puddin', if you don't stop going potty in the house Santa Claus is NOT coming to see you!" If only the threat of the absent Santa Claus would work.

Tonight, we made several trips outside for our nightly business. These trips were all successful- thank you Lord! So finally, as we're getting ready for bed- Puddin' runs into Alena's room, leaps on the bed and begins to play and pounce about. Well, I guess she got entirely too excited and...uh-oh.

With Alena's bedding now soaking wet the only alternative was for Alena to sleep in my bed with me, along with Puddin'. It felt like I was sleeping with an army of 10 people with a thousand arms and legs. On top of Puddin's twitching I now had the talking in her sleep, Alena. Needless to say, I did not get a good night's sleep.

The next morning as I'm walking into my office with dark circles and puffy eyes, someone has the audacity to tell me I look tired. My only reply was, "I have a puppy" and I just kept on walking.

I've decided our armed forces should train with puppies to fully experience the effects of sleep deprivation and how absolutely insane it can make you. After a few nights of interrupted sleep- screaming at an automated phone system makes perfectly logical sense because you are just so tired.

Puppies, like babies, should come with warning labels, instruction manuals and sedatives.

~Chapter Twelve~

There are moments that I wonder exactly who rescued who. Although Puddin' was homeless for all intensive purposes with no one to claim her, did we really rescue her or did she rescue us?

The divorce, moving to a new house and a new school has been traumatic. There have been so many tears and so much anger over the past year I can't even think about it without crying. But since Puddin' came into our lives there has been so much laughter; love; hugs and kisses. Not just with the dog but between my two-legged children as well.

We laugh when she does something funny. We all unite to chase her down when she's stolen something she shouldn't have. We all cuddle on the couch to watch tv. And all of a sudden, slumber parties in mom's bed are a regular occurrence. At least until Puddin' cuts wind and everyone bails! We all go outside to play with the dog. I thought we were happy and I guess we were. But Puddin' has heightened that happiness. She has brought us together.

Before Puddin', the nights when the kids were with my ex I was running here and there and everywhere just to avoid being alone. But now, I rush home knowing how excited she's going to be and knowing that she's going to be ready to play. She brings me such joy and calm just sitting next to me or on my lap while I rub her belly.

I kept seeing my ex-husband blissfully happy with his new girlfriend and I felt like I had to get out and start dating because that's what you're supposed to do. He can't be happy and I'm sitting here alone- that would be pathetic. I had to have someone right? But everyone I was meeting- there wasn't that spark or chemistry...they could all be great friends but I wasn't finding *that* feeling.

And I've realized that its ok to be alone because I'm not lonely. I've realized that I'm not ready for dating because for the first time in my life I'm discovering me with the help of this four-legged creature God dropped in our laps. I've rediscovered my passion for writing, with the help of Puddin'. And I am never lonely with her around.

So I ask the question again, who rescued who? If you ask me, I'd say she rescued us...and for that I will always be grateful.

~Chapter Thirteen~

The alarm goes off at 5:00a.m., there is no such thing as hitting the 'snooze' button with a puppy in the house. No way! She hears the alarm and immediately commences to bouncing about- giving kisses to be sure you're up and moving. Morning dog breath- yet another reminder of why I got divorced! I'm kidding!

So, up and out to potty we go and then it's time for breakfast as usual. The kids were with my ex last night and I think this still confuses lil' miss Puddin' sometimes. After breakfast she runs to the kid's rooms and starts scratching on the doors. I try to explain to her that the kids aren't there but that's not going to cut it. I have to open each of the kid's doors and allow her to investigate for herself.

First to Alena's room where we lunge onto the bed and proceed to snowplow through the blankets and pillows until we are thoroughly convinced there is no one hiding in the bed. She perches on the edge of the bed and looks at me standing in the doorway. This is about the time I want to say, "I told you so", but I stop myself realizing that I'm gloating....at a dog.

Now on to Brady's room. This is more of a covert military operation. I open the door and she drops her head into stealth position to peek around the corner into the room. She takes one step onto the carpet and then looks up at me, as if to ask permission. Another paw onto the carpet- another glance up at me. At this point I say, "Go ahead and look for yourself". And off like a bullet she goes, running and leaping onto the bed to repeat the snowplow

The difference in Brady's room is that after the completion of the snowplow, we have to do this roll all over the bed wildly with legs flailing in all directions as if to say, "na-nani-boo-boo I'm on your bed Brady!"

Finally she is convinced the kids aren't home and she grabs a toy and follows mom into the bathroom while I begin my morning beautification process....with a dog laying between my legs playing with her toys.

~Chapter Fourteen~

A water bug, a puppy named Puddin', a running shower and a naked Kim...what could possibly go wrong?!

WARNING! Trying to get a mental picture of the following graphic story may be disturbing to some readers. Please proceed with caution.

This morning I got into the shower and left the bathroom door open because as you know, my dog has issues and has to be able to get to her humans. So there I am in the shower when I meet a water bug in the bottom of the bathtub. I don't do bugs kind of like Puddin' doesn't do frogs. I proceed to scream and hoot and holler and jump out of the shower. This is not a pretty sight I assure you. After all, I am still a 200-pound woman that has given birth to two children. My body will never grace the cover of a magazine.

At the sound of the commotion, Puddin' races into the bathroom, ears laid back, growling and barking. She was coming to defend me against the treacherous bug. The dog that got her head stuck in a drain not too long ago; that can't go pee outside when its raining and leaps into my arms at the sight of a frog, JUMPS ferociously into the shower and commences to chase down the water bug. The shower is still going as I hadn't thought to turn it off. Everything was going fine. Well, as fine as a naked, dripping wet woman corraling a soaking wet dog chasing a water bug can be. But then, the water bug turned and started running towards Puddin'. That's when things turned ugly.

Puddin' jumps back over the bathtub wall and darts between my legs. This catches me off balance and seeing as I am soaking wet, I lose my footing and come crashing down on the floor. Puddin' gets sideswiped in the fall. I land on my big ole' butt and partly on my big ole' bad dog. I take a minute to assess if I'm truly hurt before I bust into hysterical laughter. I kept thinking, "where's the hidden camera?"

So I sit up against the wall, still naked and still wet with my sweet defender puppy sitting next to me. I look at her and am quite certain we are a sight to be seen. OK, definitely NOT a sight to be seen...EVER....by anyone. She licks my face and then looks back at the bathtub. Now, what are we going to do about that dang bug is what I am sure she was thinking because that's what I was thinking.

We finally disposed of the culprit of this morning's tragedy and I re-entered the shower. As I got back in the shower, Puddin' disappeared. I guess she had had enough nakedness for one day. I got out of the shower to find her laying on my pillows, still soaking wet from our escapade with the bug. So I took her into my bathroom with me and used the blow dryer to help dry and warm her back up.

I'm pretty sure I'm going to end up in traction or therapy before we survive the 'PPW'.

By the way, you cannot drown a water bug. Pouring water over it to force it down the drain does not work!

~Chapter Fifteen~

Entry number...heck I don't even know! My days and nights run together and I can't remember the last time I slept a solid 6 hours without being awakened by dog breath and paws on my chest.

Alena and I decided to go out for ice cream Friday night and Puddin' had to come along for the ride. Our goal is to "socialize" Puddin' and expose her to things a little at a time so she won't be so scared of everything. We go to the convenience store. I was in my pajamas so I sent Alena in while Puddin' and I waited in the car. I rolled down the window so she could smell the night air. She crawled into my lap and stuck her head gingerly out the window.

Then, some stupid, half-drunk, red-neck cowboy decides to reach in my car window to try and pet Puddin'. Well the cowardice Puddin' disappeared and the big bad pit bull came out. She nearly took the above mentioned idiot's hand right off his arm. She was growling, snarling, salivating and showing her teeth. The hair on her back was standing straight up and her ears were laid completely against her head. Said red-neck idiot says, "that's one mean pup you've got there". To which I reply, "well you reached in towards her momma uninvited and if you reach your hand in here again, I am not responsible if she bites you".

What kind of moron sticks his hand in the car of a woman, at night that: 1) he doesn't know and 2) has a mean looking dog in her lap? Clearly his cheese has done slid off his cracker! After he walked away, I praised Puddin' for protecting me. She wouldn't take her eyes off of him even after he walked away.

As soon as Alena got back in the car I rolled up the window- she crawled over into Alena's lap and resumed puppy status, complete with wagging tail.

Alena gave Puddin' a bath all by herself last week. Seeing as there were no tears, blood shed or calls to 9-1-1, I would say it was a successful venture. However, the bath will have to be repeated this week as Puddin' has decided she likes to dig and then roll in the dirt pile she creates. So now, on top of the mine field of chewed up toys in the backyard, you must now watch for holes that are deep enough to cause an ankle to snap if stepped in wrong.

How did this become my life?

~Chapter Sixteen~

We went on a walk last night and actually made it down the street. Until we met some other dogs and then it was time to go home. Success! We made it out of the yard! Woo hoo! This certainly deserved a celebration of some sort. I was thinking a milk bone or beggin' strip. Puddin' had other ideas.

Puddin' decided to celebrate by making it "snow" in my living room, hallway and bedroom. A note about chew toys- they are ALL filled with the same white fluffy stuffing. Unless you buy the unstuffed chew toy- which has a squeaker in it- which gets demolished day one- but that's another chapter in and of itself.

I took a shower and when I got out, I was amazed to find it had actually snowed in my house. Yes, the white fluffy stuff was everywhere, including hanging from Puddin's mouth. There was no doubt where the winter storm had come from. The evidence was plain as day.

Note to self: do not attempt to vacuum the white fluffy stuff. It gets stuck in the vacuum sucker hose thing because its' too light to make its way into the chamber. So while Puddin' celebrated, I sat on the kitchen floor taking apart the vacuum cleaner to clear out the "snow". Who knew I'd become so mechanically inclined?!

Further note to self: Do not attempt to take apart the vacuum cleaner while it is still turned on; still smoking or still plugged into the wall. Bad things happen. Wait until you've disconnected the power and the smoke has stopped. Also, wire coat hangers can be manipulated through the hose to retrieve the fluffy stuff. Also, a flat head screwdriver and trashcan should be readily available.

Well, puppies will be puppies and while I was fixing the vacuum cleaner, Puddin' found something else to occupy her time. I noticed it was incredibly quiet and that I had not seen her for at least 10 minutes, which is a record for my separation anxiety ridden dog. So off I went to find her. I discover my bed, bedroom and bathroom were now toilet papered. And rolling around on my bed in the toilet paper was one very happy puppy. She had actually wrapped her body in the toilet paper and was trying to eat it off of her body.

Exhausted, exasperated and incredibly annoyed, I didn't know whether to laugh or cry at the mess. I'm sure there was some cussing involved as I grabbed the trashcan and started cleaning up the latest disaster. I guess she felt pretty bad because she actually let me sleep until the alarm went off this morning and there were no accidents in the house during the night. She waited until I was getting ready and <u>after</u> she had been out to potty to have an accident in the living room. Will it ever end? Oh Lord, give me strength!

~Chapter Seventeen~

Chew toys. Where in the world would we be without toys for the dog to chew on? If you've been to a pet store recently, you will notice it is much like a kid's toy store. There are about a thousand different varieties, brands and flavors for your four-legged child to enjoy.

So here are your options. And yes, we've bought, chewed and destroyed all of them in the 'PPW':

1. The squeaky toy animal with no stuffing in it. This is GREAT! The squeaker however will make you want to cause bodily injury to someone after enough time. And if your pet is anything like Puddin' the squeaking sound requires her to whine along with it. This is even more annoying than the squeaking because they are now singing together in harmony. I would like to meet the person that thought of putting that squeaker thing in the toy and lock them in a room with about a hundred dogs and a hundred of these toys and throw away the key! The only saving grace is that Puddin' can usually destroy the squeaker on day one.

2. The stuffed animal with no squeaker. This is a quiet toy and for this reason I love it! There is no squeaking or whining when playing with this toy. There is however, the previously mentioned "snow" in your house once the toy has been mangled and shredded to pieces. That white stuffing they use to plump up the animals will now grace the floors of your home everywhere you look and make you want to sing, "I'm dreaming of a white Christmas", or take a tranquilizer...whichever works.

3. The rubber cone thing. Whoever thought of this is a genius! You stuff treats into the rubber cone and the pooch will sit for hours trying to get the treat(s) out. Its hard rubber and therefore pretty indestructible. Although, we've discovered when thrown down the hallway in an attempt to play fetch- if you step in the line of the throw- it will hurt when it hits you and will leave a nasty mark.

4. The tennis ball. Although, not its original intended purpose, the tennis ball is great for exercising your pup. You throw it- they chase it- sometimes they bring it back and sometimes they run and hide it. The problem with the tennis ball is that it bounces and if thrown in the house, is pretty much guaranteed to break a picture frame or some other knick-knack you've been treasuring for years.

5. Finally, the old trusty sock with a knot tied in it. This is truly by far my favorite toy of all time. It cannot cause me or my children bodily harm; it does not annoy the fire out of me; and it does not get destroyed. I have yet to figure out how it is still in tact. Most toys survive 2 days- tops with Puddin'. But the knot-tied sock has been around since day one. Perhaps I should mass market these. Just what the world needs, another chew-toy on the shelf at the pet store to stress new pet owners, like myself, out.

6. Rawhide bones. Great for chewing and entertaining. The downside, and I guess this is an innate instinct for dogs, is that any bone must be buried somewhere- under the couch cushions, in my closet, under the pillows on my bed. It's kind of like a treasure hunt because you never know when you are going to find the buried bone in the house. Now once you've discovered the bone, Puddin'

panics and must re-bury the bone in a new safe and secure place. In the process of frantically finding a new hiding spot for her treasure, do not get in her way. Rawhide bones across the shins; in the face or across the arms will leave bruises. Side note: if the bone is big enough and the dog is running fast enough when the bone hits you across the ribs it will knock the breath out of you...speaking from experience.

7. Nylon bones. These are amazingly indestructible! Thumbs up from Puddin's mom.

~Chapter Eighteen~

I've learned so much having Puddin' in my life. I've learned a lot about non-verbal communication. For example, if I'm irritated with her, I raise my voice ever so slightly and she gets the picture. Puddin' however, shows her frustration with me in a non-verbal way, like eating my shoes. I'll say it again- we're going to have to work on our communication if this relationship is going to survive.

However, Puddin' is very perceptive and loving when I need her to be. As you all know by now, my ex-husband has moved on with his life and yesterday, I happened across a post on social networking about how much he LOVED the new girl in his life. I cannot describe the burning in my soul I felt. Just when I thought it couldn't hurt anymore. So I did what any good jilted southern woman would do. No, I didn't grab the shotgun or a bottle of tequila. I crawled into bed and had a good old fashioned pity party. Only, Puddin' graciously accepted her invitation, curled up next to me, laid her head on my stomach and looked at me with those big green eyes that I've come to love. We laid there for at least an hour while I bawled my eyes out and never once did she move. After the tears were over it was time to get back to life. So we went and played a game of fetch in the backyard.

The rules of fetch are merely suggestions in Puddin's world. Sometimes the stick comes back and sometimes her ADD kicks in and she sees something else that peaks her interest- like an animal behind the workshop. Puddin' went to investigate and after about 3 minutes, she came racing towards me. She jumped into my lap- hitting me in the jaw, which is now black and blue, in the process. She had scratches on her belly from trying to clear through the brush in a hurry. I hugged her and reassured her she was ok and she began to lick her wounds and then it was time to play fetch again.

The moral of the story: sometimes we all need a figurative lap to climb on for a little reassurance that its going to be ok, then its time to lick your wounds and get back to living life. Who would've thought a bad puppy named Puddin' would teach me so much about life.

Daylight savings time has caused quite a bit of confusion in our house. This morning Puddin' woke me up at what I thought was 4:30a.m. to go potty and have breakfast. Well, it was actually 3:30a.m. so she ate really early this morning. Then I fell back asleep and apparently dreamt that I slept through my 5:00a.m. alarm and that the alarm I was hearing was the 6:00a.m. alarm to wake the kids up. So I jumped up, ran into the shower, got out, woke Alena and Brady up and started our morning. We were about to head out the door when Alena shouted, "MOM! It's only 6:00a.m."

Oops! Yep, these are the days of my life, as the world turns with only one life to live.

~Chapter Nineteen~

Last night I got home somewhat late (late for me at least). Puddin' and I played for a bit, went potty and then began our normal nightly routine of going to bed. Only tonight, she decided her fetch stick needed to come in the house. How can I describe this fetch-stick. I'll say it like this, a few more inches and it would be a tree branch or the Charlie Brown Christmas Tree. So the tree/ branch makes its way into the house and because its late, I just don't even care.

I don't care until she jumps into bed with the branch and whacks me in the face with it. Oh no, I am not sleeping with a tree Puddin'! I take the branch and throw it on the floor. I guess she assumed this meant I wanted to play because she did as any good dog does when a stick (or a tree) is thrown and retrieved it and brought it back to bed.

I've decided raising puppies is all about persistence and perhaps a little ignorance. I throw the branch on the floor and she brings it back again. Why didn't I assume that she would bring it back? I mean after all, that's what she did the first time. I'm a slow learner.

Finally, we compromise on the branch staying on the bed, but at the foot of the bed. She curls up next to me for a belly rub and I'm not sure who fell asleep first. I can assure you she woke up first at around 2:00a.m. I wake up to Puddin' standing over me. Her front legs are on one side of my body with her hind legs on the other side. Literally, she's standing over me. She has her face pointed towards the bedroom door. The hair on her back is standing straight up and she is growling...meanly!

As usual, I am exhausted so I let out an exasperated, "Puddin' go back to sleep!" But then I heard the knocking sound she was barking at. It sounded like someone hammering on a wall. What in the world?

We both get up to go figure out where the noise is coming from. But not before Puddin' grabs the tree, I mean the branch. I guess she was going to use it like a billystick if we happened to meet some uninvited guest in the house. That or she was ensuring that it didn't get stolen by the mysterious source of the sound. I'd like to believe it was the first scenario...but who am I kidding?

We check the house- even outside the house and cannot figure out where the sound is coming from. All the while, Puddin' is right behind me with the tree in her mouth. After a few minutes, I am too tired to care anymore and decide to give up and head back to bed.

I've told you about the race back to the bed from our middle of the night potty break right? The race wherein Puddin' tries to beat me back to the bed so she can lay in my nice warm spot before me. Well, tonight was no exception. As we turned the corner to head down the hallway Puddin' picked up her step just enough to bring herself even with me. It was dark, the hallway is narrow, my hips are wide and the dog has a tree sideways in her mouth. I don't have to tell you what happened, I'm sure you've already guessed. Fetch-stick-branch-tree across the shins; a stumbling Kim and a scared Puddin'. She's been fallen on before in the shower/ water bug incident so she was getting the heck out of the way. Fortunately, it was not necessary for me to hit the floor this night.

There was some cussing and some looks of contempt towards Puddin' as we entered my bedroom. I guess our communication is improving because she didn't even try to lay down in my spot. She dropped the tree on the floor, jumped on the bed and circled her spot.- leaving mine wide open for me to collapse into. She's learning, be it ever so slowly.

My body is beginning to resemble the mass casualty incident of fallen puppy toys in the backyard. Scratches, bruises, aches, pains and sleep deprivation. I feel like war-torn Europe some days when I look in the mirror. They say the "puppy stage" lasts up to 24 months. I did the math today. We only have 19 more months to go. I have no doubt Puddin' will survive it just fine...the question is whether I am going to survive!

~Chapter Twenty~

I know you've been anxiously awaiting the latest installment of the Puddin' stories. Things have actually been relatively calm at the house...until yesterday.

I've been brainstorming about making a headboard for my bedroom for several weeks. Finally, I found all the wood, which by the way was an absolute steal! I got all the pieces for less than $19 and you know I LOVE a bargain!

We head back home with all the wood and I pull my paints out of the closet and prepare the back patio for "my project". The kids are ecstatic and can't wait to start priming and painting. Being the forward thinking mother I am, I put cardboard down on the patio so as not to paint the patio; grab a roll of paper towels because I know we're going to need them; extra paint brushes because I know the kids won't rinse one off before dipping into another. I had it all covered.

We proceed to paint and I started with celery stalk green. It's a lovely shade of green and looks absolutely beautiful against the white-wash trim I had selected. Yes, this is going to look fabulous! I can't wait to get it finished and hanged. I digress...

So we're all having a grand time. The kids and I are painting and no one is arguing. Everyone has their own piece of wood and their own color to paint their piece. It was a lovely and rare moment in my life wherein my kids were not yelling at each other. Puddin' was entertaining herself in the yard. Truly, a wonderful moment.

Well, Puddin' is part of the family. Where we go-she goes. I've become that person that takes her dog with her to run to the ATM, to pick up the kids, etc. I've become "that" person that I used to make fun of. It's funny how life changes you.

Where I go, she goes and tonight was no different. The kids and I were on the patio and she decided that's where she needed to be. It was going well, until I got up to put my piece on the drying rack (also known as the barbeque grill).

One bottle of celery stalk green paint left open and on the ground + one precocious puppy= a guaranteed disaster!

Puddin' grabs the bottle sideways in her mouth and takes off running. The end that's open is now spilling paint everywhere! On the patio; on the white fence; on the grass; on the dog. Only it's not just spilling out of the bottle, as Puddin' turns her head side to side to see if we're chasing her, it's now slinging outwards and upwards.

I begin to yell (yes, there was some cussing involved) as I start to chase the dog. Now, how long is it going to take me to figure out that I am never going to catch her? Yet, time and time again I try to chase this dog down. As I'm yelling and running after the dog in the backyard, Alena begins to laugh hysterically. This infuriates me! After all she's the reason I have this dang dog! Brady informs me that I am _not_ using nice words and that I'm hurting Puddin's feelings, which infuriates me to the point of being ready to drop _all_ of my children off at the SPCA- the four-legged and the two-legged ones.

Finally, I catch her (only because she stopped running). I retrieved the now empty bottle of celery stalk green paint and scold the dog. This scolding causes her to prance back towards the patio- through the celery stalk green paint now covering the yard and patio and...right across the freshly painted piece of wood still sitting on the ground because I didn't make it to the barbeque grill with it. So now, there are little green paw prints everywhere and all over my project.

Things were going so well at one point in the evening.

~Chapter Twenty-One~

We've learned a valuable lesson in negotiation at our house. Almost everything is negotiable, but there are quite simply some things that <u>cannot</u> be negotiated.

Here's what happened: Brady turned 4 in September. I've been trying since September to get rid of the pacifier at bedtime. Until Tuesday, I had failed miserably at this task. Promises of ice-cream, candy or other rewards were all meaningless. Tuesday morning Brady left his pillow-pet, blanket and pacifier on the couch when we left for school. When we returned home Tuesday evening, everyone was going about their nightly routines. I was repainting the project on the back patio that Puddin' had previously attempted to "help" me with; Alena was in her fortress of solitude, also known as her bedroom, where she retreats to talk on the phone these days; Brady was watching cartoons. And Puddin', well she was making the rounds- checking on everyone.

She came out on the patio and I could hear something clanking between her teeth. I asked her what she had and I got the look of, "I didn't do it". Then, a small piece of plastic fell out of the side of her mouth while she quickly swallowed whatever was left. I picked up the tiny piece and immediately recognized it was the beloved blue pacifier. What ran through my mind was, "oh....four-letter word!"

I went to explain to Brady that Puddin' had eaten the paci and to negotiate the terms of going to bed without it tonight. After I delivered the tragic news, and yes for Brady, it was a tragic; he got up and went and squatted down at Puddin's eye level. Her tail began to wag and her hiney started to wiggle. This is, after all, a rare occasion for Brady to pay attention to her and she was so excited! I was unprepared for what came out of his mouth: "Puddin', if you'll give me back my paci, I PROMISE I'll like you".

I was left to explain that Puddin' couldn't give the paci back and even if she could, we definitely didn't want it back now. I asked him what he wanted Santa Claus to bring him this year and he said an Optimus Prime Transformer. So as we lay down for bedtime, without the paci, I assured him that if he could be my big guy and go to bed without it, that Santa would be sure to leave Optimus Prime under the tree this year.

Have you ever heard the saying, "the devil is in the details?" Well, apparently I did not adequately explain that Santa does not deliver toys until December 25th. So when Brady awoke Wednesday morning I went in to celebrate that he had slept all night without the paci and that meant he was a big guy now. Alena and Puddin' joined in the celebration because I mean, come on, this was a major event in our lives! Brady sat up in bed with all our hootin' and hollerin' and barking; and very matter of factly said, "Where's my Optimus Prime?"

Note to self: Santa will be buying Optimus Prime TODAY before the holiday rush to insure it is under the tree on Christmas morning and that it doesn't sell out, otherwise there will be you-know-what to pay come Christmas morning.

~Chapter Twenty-Two~

I really keep thinking one of these days I'm not going to have any stories to tell y'all. I'm actually looking forward to that day. Only because the experiences in all these emails are killing me, slowly but surely.

I was sitting at the computer last night working. It was a nice night so I had the back door open so Puddin' could roam while I worked. She's gotten to where she'll go outside all by herself if the door is open. She's such a big girl now.

She's lying down underneath my chair with her chin resting on my foot when she starts that growling business. I gently nudge her with my foot and tell her to hush. Like that was going to work! She crawls out from under my chair very cautiously with her head dropped low to the ground and now she is REALLY growling and staring intently at something. Ok, Puddin' what in the world is wrong now? I get up, take one step and stop.

Coming over the threshold of the doorway is the biggest, nastiest (pause for dramatic effect) TARANTULA! Not a spider an actual tarantula!

Yes, I'm sure they have their purpose here on earth and yes, I'm certain God created them for reason. However, they serve no purpose in my life and have no business being inside my house! Being home alone, what choice did I have? The creature must be executed, and I'm the one that has to do it.

I'm quite certain I looked like an electrocuted chicken as I was jumping around trying to get over being completely creeped out. While I'm still freaking out, Puddin' goes after it! She runs towards it- pounces and pushes it with her nose and then jumps back. I start hollerin', "no Puddin'!" I didn't want her to get stung or bit or whatever tarantulas do.

So I grab my flip-flops (the only pair I have left) and prepare to execute. I smash it with my flip-flop and as I'm swinging up to hit it again- the thing gets stuck to the bottom of the flip-flop. I see that although some of the creature is squashed on the floor, the majority of it is on my shoe and it's still moving! I begin to violently pound my flip-flop on the floor. Puddin' is now barking and jumping from side-to-side. It kind of reminded me of teenagers cheering on a fist fight. It was like she was saying, "get it momma- get it- kill it". Boy, I really am losing my mind! Now the dog is talking to me? Seriously?! Finally after several more whacks, the creature is dead and no, I do not feel bad about it....at all!

I wasn't about to try and clean the bottom of my flip-flop with all the bug guts and body parts now embedded on it so I just threw the whole shoe away and Puddin' was given the other flip-flop as a reward. I figure it's the least I could give her seeing as she possibly saved my life from the 8-legged intruder.

As of this morning, there is nothing left of the reward flip-flop. Another one bites the dust.

PS- there's no need for the kids to know about this...EVER...they'd never go to sleep at night if they knew.

~Chapter Twenty-Three~

I've actually met a nice man (by all accounts thus far) and I've decided to implement "the Puddin' test" while dating. In simplest terms, if the dog likes you, you can keep coming around. If she doesn't, you've got to go. The key to this being a true and reliable test is for the candidate to not know he's being tested. Otherwise, he might turn the charm on just in an effort to pass. While I am upfront that I have a dog, I don't warn them of her "issues".

To protect his privacy, we'll just call him "the boy". I had told said boy of my four-legged child. He said, "dogs love me". Well, the boy hadn't met _my_ dog. So, last night it was time for the test. I mean after all, no sense in getting too far into things with him only to find out the dog in fact, does not like him.

The boy comes through the front door. He does have a bit of an intimidating stature standing at 6'7, so I was not at all surprised when the Puddin' siren started sounding off (barking; growling; crouching in attack position; run and hide under the dining room table while still growling and barking). So far by all accounts being a respectable man, he removed his cap when he came through the door (brownie points). This quieted the siren by a decibel or two, however Puddin' was not coming out from under the table.

Me: "she doesn't like men"
Boy: "That's ok I don't either"
Me: "She'll settle down in a few minutes"
Boy: "It doesn't bother me- may I try to pet her?"
Me: "Only if you don't mind losing a limb"
Boy: "I'll take my chances"

The boy walks over to the dining room table and squats down. Puddin' comes out from under the table and races into her crate. The boy stays at her level between her crate and the dining room table for about 3 minutes before finally taking a seat on the floor.

Me: "I do have chairs. You don't have to sit on the floor"
Boy: "Your dog and I are getting to know each other. I'm fine right here"
Me: "Ok. I think I'm jealous you're paying more attention to my dog than to me"
Boy: "You don't bite- she does"
Me: "Good point"

At this juncture, the boy notices the wobbling leg on the dining room table that I haven't gotten around to fixing.

Boy: "Next time I come over let's flip this table over so I can fix that for you" (brownie points again).

So the dog and the boy are sitting there staring at each other. The boy reaches his hand out so the dog can "sniff him out". She sticks her head out of her crate, ever so carefully, smells his hand, gives it a lick and then retreats back into the crate.

Boy: "Do you have a dog biscuit or a treat?"
Me: "Of course"
Boy: "May I have one please so I can try to give it to her?" (brownie points for asking and using the word 'please' in the same sentence)
Me: "Bribery! Always works with me!"

The boy holds the biscuit in his hand and waits for her to come take it from him. This seemed to drag on forever!

Ok not really, but it felt like it. Finally, she comes out of the crate to grab the biscuit and crawls back into her crate. No more growling and barking...for the moment. The boy says, "well it's a start".

As he walks away from her, she comes out wagging her tail and following him. I inform him that he has a new friend. He turns around to look....and....back into the crate she runs beginning to bark and growl all over again.

Me: "Ok just kidding"
Boy: "It's a start and I'm in no hurry" (brownie points for appearing patient)
Me: "Yea, she's got trust issues"
Boy: "Sounds like someone else I know". (take away <u>at least</u> one set of points for calling me on MY issues)

Although the Puddin' siren never silenced completely during the boy's visit and she never did come out to let him pet her, I think with the brownie points tallied, he passed the test and can keep coming around for now. Unless he's going to keep calling me out on my issues than he totally has to be banished from the castle.

~Chapter Twenty-Four~

I got so buried with the holidays that I hadn't really thought a whole lot about writing so I'm providing a rundown of our latest exploits.

Mom was coming to visit for Christmas. Her flight didn't arrive until the middle of the night so Alena I stayed busy cleaning and cooking before it was time to leave for the airport. Since I was going to have a house full of people the next day I decided to do some baking and make my homemade cinnamon rolls. Now those that know me know that cooking is not one of my strengths, but there are a few things I make pretty darn well and cinnamon rolls is one of them.

Cinnamon rolls are a lengthy process because of the kneading and flouring and then the dough has to rise two separate times. I started the rolls at around 6:00p.m. and they were out of the oven cooling on the counter at around 9:30p.m. I told Alena, "babe, I'm going to lay down for a bit before we leave for the airport. Keep an eye on the dog and wake me up at 10:00p.m."

I go lay down in my bedroom and after about 5 minutes I hear the sound of foil crunching. I yell from my bed, "Alena, what's that sound?" As parents, sometimes we ask stupid questions we already know the answer to. I knew exactly what the sound was, but I was optimistic that I was wrong.

This is what I hear Alena say, "Puddin'! Do you know how much trouble *I'm* going to be in?!" I get up and walk into the kitchen where one very naughty puppy has demolished half of my homemade cinnamon rolls and Alena is standing there looking very disheartened and very afraid of my reaction to the pan of rolls on the kitchen floor. I'm not sure if it was exhaustion or the look on Alena's face or the way Puddin' bolted for her crate when I came around the corner, but all I could do was laugh, rather hysterically, as we began to clean up the mess.

The next day chaos fell upon our house as everyone began to arrive. My sister brought a gorgeous ham and all the sides to cook for lunch. Puddin' was socializing fairly well. It's the most people she's been around at one time since she's come to live with us, so I was a little nervous, but pleasantly surprised at her behavior.

So there we all are chatting and visiting when my sister takes the ham out of the oven and places it in the exact same spot I had placed the cinnamon rolls the night before. You already know what happened next. While no one was looking, Puddin' pulled the entire ham and platter onto the floor and decided to help herself. We heard the clash of the platter hitting the floor and I knew what had happened. Only this time, she didn't bolt for her crate. She was eating as much as possible, for as long as possible. That night I had a puppy with a very upset tummy given all the rich "people" food she had ingested in two days.

I think mom was a bit surprised at Puddin's size. She's not a little pup anymore. She's pushing 50 pounds these days. Although she doesn't realize how big she is and has no problem barreling into your lap at full speed or pouncing on you in the morning if you are still sleeping and she's ready to play. The world revolves around Puddin' at our house, didn't you know?

Puddin' ate one of mom's earrings that was accidentally left within reach. It was not a major event for us because she eats all sorts of things she's not supposed to all the time. We just chalk it up as another Puddin' catastrophe. Mom, however really liked those earrings and actually asked me to check the backyard for the earring. As you know- what goes in must come out eventually. I love my mom. But there are some things that I am just NOT going to do. I'll buy her a new pair and call it a day.

Puddin' loves her crate, but it was obvious with her weight gain and recent growth spurt that it was time for a new, bigger crate. Crates are outrageously expensive in my opinion. But with a puppy, they are a necessity. So I shop for a week and finally found a reasonably priced one at the local "get it all in one stop" store. And much to Alena's satisfaction, a portion of the purchase price of the crate is donated to the ASPCA. So we did a little good too. I feel so much better about the $100+ I spent, don't you?

So there I am at the store looking for the crate. Of course, all the smaller sized crates are on the bottom racks. The large/ extra-large crate I need is on the top rack and there is not an employee in sight anywhere! Now, why in the world would you put the heavy, big, bulky ones on the top rack and the smaller more compact ones on the bottom? Sounds like a lawsuit waiting to happen if you ask me! As my sister says, "the dumb suffer" and perhaps I'm dumb for having a big ole' dog and part of my suffering is reaching high for the right sized crate. Who knows!

I stand up on one of those wooden pallet things to reach the top rack and start pulling a crate down when a nice man walks by. Here I'm thinking, oh thank goodness! Surely chivalry isn't dead and this man is going to help me. Well he stops and says, "lady, are you sure you need that big of a crate, I mean what kind of dog do you have?"

I hate this question. I despise this question. I cringe when I hear it. I've come to react this way because of the look and responses I get once I answer it. I respond, "pit bull", as I'm still trying to pull the crate off the shelf. The man says, "oh...well...good luck" and walks away leaving me to pull the crate down almost on top of my head. Chivalry is alas, MIA!

A larger crate means a bigger blanket of some sort right? I find this lovely dog bed that will fit perfectly inside the new crate. It's cushioned and padded and soft and fluffy. Why did I think it was a good idea? I don't know. But I splurged and bought the mutt the $30 bed. After all, this dog has brought so much happiness to my home, it's the least I can do. Haha!

I get the crate and the dog bed home and she seems to like them both. The next day we leave Puddin' in her crate when everyone leaves. I get a call from mom that evening because she was the first one home and this is how the conversation started: "Kim, (giggle, giggle) I hope you weren't attached to that new dog bed because there is green fuzz EVERYWHERE! (giggle, giggle)". Yep, she demolished the new bed in less than 24 hours. Only this time, I had green "snow" instead of the usual white fluffy stuff in the kitchen.

I've started actually putting the manuscript for the book together on my laptop. Last night I was sitting in bed typing while Puddin' was laying down next to me. She's so sweet sometimes. Wait! I spoke too soon. I guess Puddin' decided since the book is about her, she needed to help me write it. So there I am typing away, I pause and reach for a drink from my diet coke on the nightstand. When I look back around, Puddin' is now standing on the keyboard and the page is filled with something like this:

'Alksj;oifosducpiopautu4o5u30qirlfy93452-3uhrflnsdsfuoupjspfosioufoufoh'

Wow! That ought to make for some interesting reading. I thought about leaving it and putting an author's note stating: "From Puddin' with love". But instead, I just hit 'save' and called it a night because it was obvious I wasn't getting anything else written.

It's not all bad all the time though. She sleeps through the night nowadays and as long as I get up when she's ready in the mornings, we don't have any accidents in the house. Now, if we could get her to quit jumping on people and putting her paws on the kitchen counter and eating off of unattended plates left around, I'd be happy.

As the saying goes, "Rome wasn't built in a day". But have you ever noticed that rarely do people reference the collapse of Rome? I wonder why?

~Chapter Twenty-Five~

Did you know you can buy a book called, "First Aid for Dogs for Dummies" at the pet store? I know what you're thinking, just how do I know this? Well, I'm so glad you asked!

I got home last night and things were NOT normal. Puddin' was sitting at the very back of her crate. There was no wagging tail or smiling face. Yes, my dog smiles. Instead, there were shards and pieces of black plastic all over the floor surrounding her crate and blood...quite a bit of it, but not enough to call the crime scene or the puppy ambulance. I got her out of her crate to discover she had torn up the plastic bottom of her crate and in doing so the sharp edges of the plastic had cut her belly.

I clean her up as best I can and determine they are all superficial cuts and nothing that requires immediate medical attention. In my infinite wisdom as a now seasoned pet owner, I cleaned her off with hydrogen peroxide and put Neosporin on the cuts. That's what I'd do for my two-legged children so I figured it couldn't hurt for Puddin'. She would not stop licking her wounds no matter how hard I tried to stop her.

Off we go to the local pet store to see if there's something over the counter and maybe specific to pets I should use instead. I took Puddin' with me so I wouldn't have to try to describe it to the folks there. My favorite person wasn't working. This should've been my first clue to just go back home. I don't even know this kid's name but he is my absolute favorite associate at this store! He knows

Puddin' was an unexpected blessing and that she has issues. He knows that I'm new to puppy ownership and he knows that I am incredibly cheap and have my own set of issues. Knowing all of this, he is kind, understanding and non-judgmental. Thus, the reason he is my favorite person at this store!

Well as I said, he wasn't there. I should've just gone home but one of my children was hurt. I couldn't just go home. A young lady asked if she could help me. I tell her very briefly what happened while Puddin' is still licking her ouchies like crazy in the middle of the store entrance. The young lady says, "did you put anything on these cuts?" Me: "Yes, I cleaned them hydrogen peroxide and then put Neosporin on them". She doesn't say anything, not-a-word. She reaches towards the rack behind her and hands me "First Aid for Dogs for Dummies" and walks away. I'm relatively certain I've just been insulted and this is her way of calling me a complete idiot. I tried not to take it personally. I politely took the book from her and as she walked away, I caught myself saying, "thank you". Boy! Did those words taste like crap coming out! I proceeded to the checkout line. A half a gallon of gas and a few minutes of humiliation later, we were on our way home.

So here's what I learned. Apparently allowing the dog to lick their wounds is how they heal. There is something about their saliva that is medicinal and putting anything over the wound, like Neosporin, prohibits the saliva from doing its job. Not to mention, it's not good for them to ingest it. In fact, on the tube of Neosporin it says, "for external use only". This means do not ingest it. Apparently, this applies to four-legged fur balls as well as two-legged knuckleheads.

Leaving "First Aid for Dogs for Dummies" on the bed when you fall asleep reading it insures that it will be shredded and destroyed during the night. I guess Puddin' didn't think too highly of the material. I cannot give an opinion as I only read the chapter on cuts before its demise.

And in case you didn't know, there are a million websites on animal first aid. Everything from traditional medicine; homeopathic remedies; aromatherapy and....music therapy for dogs! Seriously?

~Chapter Twenty-Six~

As colorful as I can be, I just really cannot adequately describe or explain the circumstances of the following. Me, as my daughter has nicknamed me, "the mouth of the south", cannot come up with the words. Meaning, quite possibly, for the first time in my life...I am speechless. There are two things I never in my life expected to hear myself say to my children.

<u>#1: Keep your tongues in your own mouths and to yourselves</u>. Yes, I actually had to say this to my two-legged children that were imitating Puddin's kisses. Only the one getting "kissed" did not like it and calling in that exasperated tone and annoyed pitch, "MOM!" made the above statement necessary.

<u>#2: Who peed on my bed?</u> Here again, I outwardly ask the question I already know the answer to. This momentary lapse in judgment wherein my mouth speaks before my brain engages causes my offspring to think I am not exactly the brightest crayon in the box and laugh uncontrollably at me. However, in my defense, on this particular occasion I'm not exactly sure who the culprit was...Brady and Puddin' both looked equally suspect and guilty.

Happy Wednesday!

~Chapter Twenty-Seven~

This morning I was in the shower (no worries there is no need for a graphic reader's warning as with the water bug incident). Puddin' was chillin' out on the bathmat. Chillin' out quite simply means she was laying there like a bump on a log. I hear a bit of commotion so I pull back the shower curtain to see what she's gotten into. Anytime there is an unusual sound in the house, Puddin' has gotten a hold of something she shouldn't have so I'm never too anxious to see what it is. When I pulled the shower curtain back all I could see was Puddin' sitting on the bathmat with my towels lying on the floor and somewhat on top of her. No big deal- she pulled my towels off the rack. I go back to my shower and finish up.

I step out of the shower and reach for my towel (now on the floor). Only now she's sitting on it and isn't in a big hurry to move. I pull the towel while trying to push her off of it at the same time. She's being stubborn and reluctant to move for some reason. Me: "Ok Puddin' enough- MOVE!" She finally moves and I discover where she had been sitting on top of the fluffy white bathmat were globs of fuchsia colored lip gloss...the goopy kind that comes in a squeeze tube. "Dang it Puddin'!" At this point, she turns and tucks her tail and slivers somewhat cowardly to my bedroom.

I wrap the towel around me, take the bathmat to the laundry room, spray it with some stain remover, drop it in the washer with some bleach and start the machine. I head to my bedroom to start getting ready for work. Oh well, all is well that ends well right? Nope, we ain't done yet...

I forgot to mention that I washed my hair this morning. This means I grab two towels and because of the outrageous amount of hair on my head, one towel is solely dedicated to wrapping my wet hair. I'm in my bathroom when I unravel the towel from my head and begin to comb through it...only my hair is sticky. I look at my hair towel to discover gobs of the same fuchsia lip gloss all over it. Wait, you mean to tell me I now have goopy fuchsia lip gloss in my hair, which means I'm going to have to re-wash my hair? Yep, that's <u>exactly</u> what that means.

As I walk by the dog lying on my bed, I mutter something not very nice in her general direction. She perks her head up and follows me into the bathroom. I drop the lip gloss tainted towel in the laundry hamper as we walk by it; I hang my "body" towel on the hook and re-enter the shower to re-wash my hair.

I exit the shower for the second time this morning- grab my towel off the hook- wrap it around me and grab a fresh towel out of the cabinet for my hair. I go back to getting ready for work and as I unwrap the towel from around my body to get dressed...yep, you guessed it...fuchsia lip gloss all over me!

Now, I know what you're thinking... Did she not notice it the first time she got back in the shower? Did she not think to check the body towel since the hair towel had lip gloss on it? Here's my defense- I have a head cold and feel like crud so perhaps my thinking isn't exactly clear right now.

So back to the bathroom- drop towel in hamper- re-enter shower for now my third shower of the morning. I did make it to work on time...although I'm not sure how. I did not find the tube of lip gloss so that has me a bit concerned as to what I may find when I get home this evening, but I can't think about that or I might never go back home.

When will it end?

~Chapter Twenty-Eight~

Alena had a fast lesson in Biology and Economics this week, thanks to Puddin'. Puddin' is now 7 months old and is a female pup...so it was about "that" time as I haven't had her fixed yet. So here's how the phone conversation went yesterday when Alena got home from school:

Receptionist at my office: "Kim, Alena's on the phone"
Me, picking up the phone: "Hi Babe. How was your day?"
Alena: "Hi Mom. What does it mean when Puddin's thing is red?"
Me: "What thing are you talking about?" Another brilliant parental moment wherein I ask a question I already know the answer to.
Alena: "You know!"
Me: "Oh well, it means she's in heat. It's not a big deal. Just be sure if she tries to lay on any of the furniture you put a towel down. I'll stop and get doggy diapers on my way home."
Alena: "Ewwwww!!! That's disgusting!!! YOU need to get her fixed."

Biology lesson over, let's move on to Economics...

Me: "Babe, I know but I don't have the almost $300 it cost to have her fixed right now."
Alena: "Oh. Well, let's have a lemonade stand- $300 a glass."
Me: "Alena who in the h-e-double-hockey-sticks do you know that's going to pay $300 for a glass of lemonade?"
Alena: "Neena and Aunt Pat".

Here endeth today's lessons.

~Chapter Twenty-Nine~

You know the old biblical saying about, "he who spareth the rod spoileth the child?" Well, I've decided this applies to dogs as well. We were so careful to love and comfort lil' miss Puddin' when she came into our lives because she had obviously not been treated kindly previously, so much so that the rules of the house became merely suggestions for her. Needless to say and as evidenced by all the stories I've shared, much like with children turning into out of control teenagers, I was beginning to have an out of control dog.

She was jumping on top of the furniture; on top of people; barking incessantly any time she heard a noise- which with my new neighbors across the street partying until all hours of the morning is a bit annoying at 3am. The noise from the parties is tolerable...but I can't handle being woken up by a barking dog- it makes my heart jump out of my chest. As usual, I digress...

There's the ever present chewing anything and everything she can get her paws on; the "I'll show you" potty in the house when the backdoor is wide open for her to do her business outside; the "you're not paying enough attention to me so I'm going to destroy something to get your attention" antics. It was beginning to really weigh on me emotionally, physically and perhaps mentally as well.

I don't necessarily believe in corporal punishment, but Puddin' had pushed me to my breaking point. She had once again jumped up onto the counter to retrieve the people food left within her reach. There was some yelling of Puddin's name followed by some, "Why do we have this dang dog"! Ok, time to regroup mom and come up with an effective training tool to whip Puddin' into shape. After all, the dog DOES NOT rule this house. I am the human, it's time to retake my control here...

One rolled up newspaper pointed at her (ok actually two- one in the living room and one on my nightstand- don't want to have to go huntin' one down when I need it. Come to think of it, I may need to collect a few more and keep them in every room in the house...hmmm) and one "NO" in a stern voice means one very obedient Puddin'. Anytime Puddin' gets to acting wild or out of line, all I have to do is grab one of the rolled up newspapers and point it at her. She immediately stops what she's doing and sits down. Or runs to her crate and lays down with this, "I'm really sorry" look on her face.

Why didn't I think of this months ago? I think about all the tragedies that could've been avoided had I utilized this from the beginning. After all, she is like a child and what kids need is the security of discipline. I'm sure there's some psycho babble reasoning behind why kids push us to ensure we push back...but that's WAY beyond my level of education or understanding. I just know that when my kids push me- I push back so it was time to apply this principle with Puddin'.

~Chapter Thirty~

Boundaries...the word can have so many interpretations, definitions and meanings in life. But with Puddin' the word, for all intensive purposes, it is meaningless and non-existent.

Little things like, don't jump up on the counter to retrieve people food- nope. Or, Puddin', I don't want you on top of my chest licking my face- no luck. Or, Puddin' I don't need you jumping in my lap while I'm sitting on the porcelain throne- not a chance. Or, Puddin' you really don't need to walk across the back of the couch and fall on my head when I'm sitting enjoying some good trash tv- forget it! It seems the only boundary Puddin' respects, is the entrance to Brady's room and even THAT is debatable at times.

We've tried, repeatedly to stop her from crawling under Alena's bed since she gets stuck and then whines incessantly and annoyingly. When she ignores the under the bed boundary, we have to undergo the process of freeing Puddin'. And it is a process indeed!

Here's how it usually goes...

Alena yells, "Mom! Puddin's stuck under the bed again". I exasperatedly stop whatever I am doing to begin the process of un-stucking (I know it's not a word, but it works) the dang dog. I walk into Alena's room where she is rather annoyed at the amount of time it took me to get there. We assume the position and Alena and I lift the bed. I get enough of a grip to hold it up by myself (not easy) while she squats down to convince Puddin' to come out (again, not easy), this usually takes a few minutes.

Do you know how hard it is to make your voice sound sweet and calm when you are absolutely and completely irritated? There's some, "you stupid dog- come on"! Followed by some, "Alena get her out from there this bed is getting heavy"! Responding with, "Mom I'm trying! What do you want me to do"?! This results in my "Don't you take that tone with me young lady"! And Alena's "Well, I'm not the one that put her under there. Why are you mad at me"?! The longer this takes the more our volume and our tempers escalate.

No wonder the dang dog won't come out- her owners are crazy!

The only smart one in the bunch is Brady...he stays clear of the commotion. But maybe that's because he could really care less if the dog is stuck under the bed...as long as she doesn't have one of his toys.

During a thunderstorm, this process takes even longer. And because of last night's storms, unfortunately for us, this was a process we had to repeat multiple times until about 11:00pm. At that point, we gave up on keeping her out from under the bed and just decided to let her be stuck. Amazingly, Puddin' managed to free herself and climb onto the bed with Alena and sleep comfortably...on top of her. Sneaky little devil she is. Which begs the question, why do we put ourselves through this time and time again when she is obviously capable of freeing herself? Well, I never said we were the sharpest knives in the drawer.

~Chapter Thirty-One~

Anyone that knows me knows that I like a clean and organized house. I get myself worked into a tizzy when things are out of order or discombobulated. Puddin' has taught me that there are more important things than a clean and organized house- like going outside and throwing the stick or doing tricks for treats or gobs of unwanted kisses because she's just so tickled we're finally home. And that sometimes the most fun of all is creating the mess! Yes, the dishes, dusting, vacuuming, laundry can all wait until after playtime. Perfection is impossible and this was never more evident than when I walked into Alena's room this morning to investigate a noise.

I was getting ready for work when I heard this unusual sound. I walked out of my bathroom, and listened to determine where the sound was coming from. It then dawned on me that Puddin' had not come in to visit me like she usually does while I'm putting my make-up on. This can't be good. I walk into Alena's room and do a quick glance over the bed to locate Puddin' in the blankets somewhere. Nope, not there. Then I hear the scratching sound again...it was coming from under the bed.

I get down on my hands and knees and look under the bed. There she was, laying on her back clawing and chewing apart the bottom of the box springs. There was white gauzy stuff and strips of fabric everywhere! She turned her head and looked at me with those perked ears and gauze hanging from her mouth. The look was one of, "oh boy, how much trouble am I in".

Now, I can scream and hoot and holler and wake up the kids, who are still fast asleep. All because I'm irritated at the mess I am now going to have to clean up and to make a point to sweet Puddin' that I am NOT happy with her. Or, I can accept that perfection in my home is unattainable anymore and pull a Scarlet O'Hara and worry about it tomorrow.

Because my life has taught me to pick my battles...I just walked away. I left Puddin' to demolish the bottom of the bed; I let the kids continue to sleep peacefully and I went back to getting ready for work. I am dreading going to home in awhile to clean up the mess.

On another note, while somewhat inappropriate- it is completely hilarious if you can picture the scene in your mind...

Puddin' has graduated dog food recently and this has caused some "cutting the wind" incidents. Most dogs have the ability to clear a room and Puddin' is no different. Although, usually they are the silent ones...the ones you don't know they've cut loose until you are gagging as you bolt from the room.

Saturday morning we were sitting on the couch while I was enjoying a cup of coffee. It was a calm morning and I was waiting for the kids to come home. Puddin' decided to get up and stretch and as she did, she let one rip...only it was not silent...it kind of hissed and made that flubber sound (I really can't think of another word to describe it).

Well, at the sound of "the wind", she immediately turned her head towards her rear-end and started growling at her own butt! Oops, there goes another one. She jumps off the couch and starts alternating between growling and barking...while chasing her own backside. I'm sitting on the couch, spilling coffee all over my pajamas, which are already wet because...well I'm laughing hysterically and I've had two kids...some things just don't hold anymore. I can't stop laughing to calm her down and convince her that her butt is NOT trying to hurt her. She'd calm down and then here comes another one and the whole process of attacking the source of the noise commences again!

Finally, she gave up seeing the fight was futile. Now, when she cuts wind that has noise accompanying it, there's a slight "gruff" and a glance at her hiney before she goes back to doing whatever is was she was doing before the rude interruption.

~Chapter Thirty-Two~

Puddin' has actually been behaving herself rather well...Thus it's been pretty boring around our house. Although- last night got a little interesting...

I had company over for a bit. And in typical fashion, we will protect his identity and just refer to him as, "Bob". Don't ask me where "Bob" came from. It's just the first fake name I could come up with. Since "Bob" is an appropriate age, I can't very well refer to him as "the boy". So, "Bob" it is.

Puddin' actually liked "Bob". She barks and growls until she realized it's him and then her tail starts wagging as she runs to jump on him. She plays with him and lets him pet her and hug on her. She'll play fetch with him- which is a delicate subject since I can't even get her to return the fetch stick to me, but nevertheless, they seem to get along well. We decided to take Puddin' out for some exercise in the backyard. It has rained recently so the yard is still muddy in some areas. But it was a nice night and not too cold so out we went. The fetch stick was thrown, retrieved and repeated several times and then...the appeal of the mud distracted lil' miss Puddin' and she simply could not resist rolling around in it; flailing her body this way and that way insuring full body coverage.

Of course as soon as she was done rolling in the mud she bolted into the house through the backdoor, which I had inadvertently left wide open. Mud covered Puddin' runs into the house with Kim and "Bob" in hot pursuit to catch her before she hit the carpet. We contain her in the kitchen long enough to get a towel and start wiping her off. While we were toweling her off, "Bob" removed her collar to get the mud underneath it. He placed the collar on the kitchen floor and we both completely forgot about it.

"Bob" went home and as Puddin' and I were going to bed, I hear this clanking sound in her mouth followed by a big ole' gulp. I turn the night light back on to see what she's eaten this time, to find only her tag and a sliver of the camo cloth collar remaining, hanging from her mouth. She had eaten the majority of her collar, plastic clasp and all.

I guess if I still owned my copy of ""First Aid for Dogs for Dummies" I would know whether this constituted an emergency trip to the vet. But, because I know my dog and this is by far not the worst thing she's eaten, I just took the remains of the collar, rolled over and went to sleep.

So I suppose I'll be running back to the pet store, again, on my lunch break, again, today to buy another collar AND some new chewing toys apparently.

~Chapter Thirty-Three~

Just when I think this dang dog and I cannot possibly have any more "adventures" together, she proves me wrong.

Saturday evening I decided since I had the house to myself, to take a long hot bubble bath, complete with candles and some great meditation music. I had left the door to the bathroom open so that I wouldn't have to get out of the bath to open the door when Puddin' started flailing her body against it to get in. I left the backdoor open so she could go outside and say hello to her friends; explore; run; dig; whatever. I gave her a rawhide bone and filled a "kong" with peanut butter all to keep her occupied while I relaxed in my personal spa created atmosphere.

Puddin' came to visit a time or two without incident. She'd come in, sit by the bathtub until I acknowledged her and then would go back to playing. I was thoroughly enjoying soaking in the bath without, "Mom can I; or mom, will you; or mom"! It was all going well. I had taken the necessary precautions to ensure Puddin' would not get bored and get into trouble thus allowing me to enjoy my peace and serenity.

In typical Murphy's Law fashion, about the time I was truly relaxed I heard the hurried clacking of Puddin's paws on the wood floor. I knew something was wrong...something had spooked her. Maybe there was a frog on the back porch or maybe a squirrel...the world will never know. I heard the attempted halting of her paws, as she tried to round the corner too quickly and slid into the wall. I heard her stand back up and the clacking begins again as she tries to gain enough traction to resume her run...around the corner. I see her coming in full gallop towards me. Surely she's going to stop...surely. Nope. She charges towards the bathtub, jumps over the bathtub wall and into the bath with me. Waves of water cascade over the side of the bathtub onto the floor. Candles are knocked over in the Tsunami like waves. Wax is now all over the floor, along with about half of the water from my bath. Puddin' is splashing and panting as she tries to get her footing and I am trying to move out of her way. Her claws feel like knives digging into my body, as she tries to stand.

I manage to pull myself out of the bath and grab a towel. I know I've been lonely recently, but dang! Bathing with a dog is NOT exactly the intimate experience I was hoping for. I mean I prefer those kind of experiences to be shared with someone of the two-legged, male persuasion. Momma would say beggars can't be choosers, but I would have to disagree in this instance. There's nothing like feeling violated by your dog!

As I am wrapping the towel around me; picking up the candles and throwing towels on the floor to mop up the water; Puddin' is thoroughly enjoying what's left of my bath. She's rolling around; drinking the water; panting and smiling. She has bubbles on her head and looks so dang cute I can't do anything but laugh.

I clean up the mess and of course, about the time all the water is mopped up, Puddin' decides she's had enough of bath time and jumps out and shakes the water off of her. At this point, I give up. I put on my pajamas, close the back door, blow out the remaining candles and go to bed. When and if this compilation of stories ever makes it to publishing, I'm thoroughly convinced I am going to have to write it under an assumed identity to preserve what little dignity I have left!

I believe Winston Churchill once said, "Never Give Up! Never Surrender"! Well, he never met Puddin'. And if he did, I do believe history would be written quite differently.

~Chapter Thirty-Four~

Today marks day 145 since Puddin' became a part of our family. 145 days...4.5 months...It seems like a lifetime ago and I honestly cannot remember what life was like without her around. The battles over toys being chewed; the potty training; the nights she's gotten into something; stuck under the bed; all of the bruises and scratches; the sleepless nights all seemed insignificant this morning.

Brady has been sleeping with his bedroom door closed because he doesn't like Pudidn' coming into his room. You all know this by now. Last night, as I tucked him in, he said, "Mom, you can leave my door open- its ok for Puddin' to come in". While I thought it strange, I honored his wishes and left his door open.

I woke up several times last night for some reason. I made my usual rounds to be sure the kids were warm enough. My first time up was around 11:20pm. I checked on Alena and found her and Puddin' sound asleep nose to nose. I kind of snickered and went to check on Brady. He looked like a rolly-poley since he had kicked all of his blankets off. I put the blankets back over him and went back to sleep.

At 4:14am, I woke up again and made the rounds again. I check on Alena- she was still fast asleep, Puddin' however was not in her bed. Hmmm...I go into Brady's room and find Puddin' laying right next to Brady and Brady's arm draped over her. Puddin' is awake. She just looks at me. She never raises her head, wags her tail or moves.

Brady wakes up at 5:30am and calls to me from his room. I go in to tell him good morning. Puddin' is now licking him and wagging her tail incessantly. Brady is laughing one of those deep belly laughs; the kind of laugh that you can't help but join in. Brady: "Puddin' that's enough! I love you Puddin'!" Me: "Brady you like Puddin' now?" Brady: "Mommy, I love Puddin'. She sleeped with me 'cuz I had a yucky dream. An' I like Puddin' sleepin' wit' me- but she can't be wild."

My lesson in life for today: Sometimes love comes softly and slowly. It's not always instant affection and fireworks. Sometimes, there are people (or dogs) in our lives on the outside circumference of our "circle" that you don't realize are there or how much they care...until they step up when you need them. So for today, I will be grateful for those circumference people (or dogs) and the role they play in my life.

Happy Carnival!!

~Chapter Thirty-Five~

Time and time again I find myself asking the same question, "who rescued who?"

Last week was NOT a good week...Wednesday my wallet and cell phone were stolen. Besides feeling angry, I felt very threatened and insecure. After all, the thief now had my driver's license with my home address on it. For a single woman living alone, this kind of privacy violation shook me to my core...figuratively and literally.

I think sometimes in today's world of technology our friendships have become sterile, for lack of a better word. With communication being primarily via electronic means, our relationships have become virtual instead of real. While I'm grateful for electronic media to allow me to keep in touch with friends and family that aren't here, sometimes you need the face-to-face time of a friend. A hug, a pat on the shoulder, human touch cannot be replaced or replicated in cyberspace. You can communicate through cyberspace, but sometimes it's difficult to connect.

So if I learned anything from last week's experiences, I hope it's that I make more of an effort to spend real time with friends and loved ones when I can, instead of relying on virtuality.

Wednesday evening, I was able to get that face-to-face time with some close friends that knew I needed them. Although I am grateful for their contact, I am most grateful for the comfort and security I felt from lil' miss Puddin'. I have become one of those crazy dog people...Lord help me!

I got home Wednesday evening and she was very eager to see me. We played a round of Puddin' fetch in the backyard, had some peanut butter and then had some cuddling time on the bed. I had no idea how loving on Puddin' while I sat and had a good cry on my bed about the day's events could be so cathartic.

She looked at me with those big green eyes as if she understood. She tried to lick the tears off my face, which totally grossed me out, but I appreciated the sentiment. She laid right next to me with her head resting on my stomach all night. She didn't move, except to raise her head when she heard a sound. Neither of us slept...as long as I was awake, she was awake. And I was grateful for the companionship, the love, affection and security of knowing she would sound the Puddin' siren at the first sign of trouble.

Who would've ever thought this four- legged creature would make such an impact on my life! I will have to agree with something someone said awhile back, in that I needed Puddin' as much as she needed me.

Here's hoping this week is less eventful. Alena has her first track meet on Thursday. She's running the hurdles and throwing the discus...or maybe it's the shot-putt...I can't remember! I prefer the indoor climate controlled sports to those outdoor sports, but at least she's staying active. Brady has decided he wants to take karate...just what I need: a four-year-old that can whoop my rear-end! Oh well!

~Chapter Thirty-Six~

I have decided that when I grow up I want to be just like lil' miss Puddin'. I want to be allowed to growl and bark and snarl at people I do not like. Sometimes trying to be the bigger better person after a divorce just plain sucks! I wonder if she might be able to get away with taking a chunk out of somebody's butt and blame it on her not knowing any better because she's a puppy...just once...maybe twice? Hmmm... Line 'em up! Haha!

In all seriousness though, the dang dog has it made! She doesn't have to do anything! She gets to play when she wants to. Annoy the heck outta ya' 'til she gets her belly rubbed. Someone else prepares her food and cleans up after her AND she gets to nap whenever she dang well pleases. This dog has the life and I want to be her when I grow up.

Puddin' and I were arguing over the blankets before bed Saturday night. I was trying to climb under them while she was trying to lay on top of them. It was a bit of a tug-of-war, but I won. Momma always said persistence pays off. Ok, fine I threw the bone down the hallway and while she was chasing it, I climbed under the blankets and claimed my spot. Geesh!

We were sleeping peacefully. Ok not so peacefully seeing as I woke myself up snoring on more than one occasion and Puddin' had a gassy tummy. But at this particular moment, we were sleeping peacefully until I was awakened by the Puddin' siren. I tried the usual gentle push with my foot to silence her, but it wasn't working. The more I pushed, the louder she got. I sat up and her head darted from me to the bedroom doorway and back at a rapid pace. I guess she was telling me we needed to go check out whatever was causing her alarm.

Off we go into the dark to investigate. Now why is it I have this big ole' bad a** "aggressive" breed dog and anytime we go to investigate something in the night, she walks behind me? I've said it before and I'll say it again, aggressive breed my butt!

When we approached the kitchen I remembered I had started the dryer before going to bed. Puddin' darted for the laundry room and began to growl, bark and jump towards the dryer. Well thank the Lord she's aggressive enough to kill the dryer!

I tried to reassure her that the dryer was NOT trying to attack me or break into the house, seeing as it's already IN the house...no luck. I finally gave up reasoning with her and this is when I realize my mental sanity has finally slipped away because I am attempting to reason...with a dog...in the middle of the night...in my pajamas...over a dryer. Nope, no sanity left here.

I turn the dryer off and it's the race back to the bedroom for the warm spot...at least this time she climbed under the blankets.

~Closing Thoughts~

I watched an ASPCA commercial the other night about dogs that are abandoned and left in city pounds to be euthanized. These commercials never bother me but since Puddin' was resting her head in my lap at this moment, I realized that could've been her. And I wondered how many other people's lives had been changed by the unexpected blessing of a runaway, abandoned or shelter pet.

On the dark and probably completely politically incorrect side of things, I think about how much money I've spent on puppy food; shots and medical care; puppy toys and accessories; puppy treats; professional boarding when I travel, I feel like I am doing my part to stimulate the economy in these times of recession! Albeit, the pet industry economy. Regardless of how much money I've spent I can honestly say the rewards far outweigh the monetary cost.

As I stated previously, this story started off as emails to my mom and friends to make them laugh at the antics of having a puppy in the house. I had no idea that this journey would entwine major life lessons with puppyhood, for lack of a better word. I had no idea that writing these emails would be a journey of healing for me.

I truly believe that sometimes there are things in life that can only be explained as divine intervention. I believe sometimes God gives us what we need and not necessarily what we want, because He knows what's best for us. Why did God bring Puddin' to our home? That first night I had no clue!

Now, when I look into that sweet dog's eyes I see love, patience, tolerance, laughter, compassion and companionship. I thought I knew about these things but it took bad reputation pit bull named Puddin' coming to live with us for me to fully grasp them. God truly puts people, places, situations and perhaps even puppies in our paths for us to learn and grow.

As Puddin' grows physically and matures- be it ever so slowly- I grow too. I grow stronger every day and she teaches me something new almost daily. So the moral of the story for today- every experience can be a learning opportunity if we allow it to be. Never stop growing. Remain teachable so that God can work with and in you.

I used to believe that God gave us teenagers to drive us to our knees in prayer. Well, the teenage years are fast approaching and perhaps God gave me Puddin' so I can start practicing.

For more information about Puddin', contact her at:
Facebook: Puddin' Johnston
Twitter: @puddin_johnston
Instagram: puddinjohnston

Email: thepuddindiaries@gmail.com